Pink Toys, Yes or No

Lin Picou

Educational Media

rourkeeducationalmedia.com

*Scan for Related Titles
and Teacher Resources*

Teaching Focus:
Using Expression- Have students read aloud to practice reading with expression and with appropriate pacing.

Before Reading:

Building Academic Vocabulary and Background Knowledge
Before reading a book, it is important to set the stage for your child or students by using pre-reading strategies. This will help them develop their vocabulary, increase their reading comprehension, and make connections across the curriculum.

1. *Read the title and look at the cover. Let's make predictions about what this book will be about.*
2. *Take a picture walk by talking about the pictures/photographs in the book. Implant the vocabulary as you take the picture walk. Be sure to talk about the text features such as headings, Table of Contents, glossary, bolded words, captions, charts/ diagrams, or Index.*
3. *Have students read the first page of text with you then have students read the remaining text.*
4. *Strategy Talk – use to assist students while reading.*
   - Get your mouth ready
   - Look at the picture
   - Think…does it make sense
   - Think…does it look right
   - Think…does it sound right
   - Chunk it – by looking for a part you know
5. *Read it again.*
6. *After reading the book complete the activities below.*

Content Area Vocabulary
Use glossary words in a sentence.
discourage
feminine
opponents
proponents
relatives
separately

After Reading:

Comprehension and Extension Activity
After reading the book, work on the following questions with your child or students in order to check their level of reading comprehension and content mastery.

1. *Why might someone like the color pink? (Summarize)*
2. *Why might boys think the color pink is for girls? (Infer)*
3. *Do you have anything that is pink? Do you have anything blue? Is the color of something important to you? (Text to self connection)*
4. *How can someone feel left out of playing if they think pink is just for girls or blue is just for boys? (Asking questions)*

Extension Activity
Think about your favorite toy store. Many have a girls' section and a boys' section. Gender-equal means that it doesn't matte who plays with the item. Choose a toy that you play with. Is it sold to boys or to girls? What on the package or item makes it feel more boyish or girlish? Think of ways that a package or item can be gender-equal so that all kids will want to play with it.

Table of Contents

Introduction

"I want the pink toy!"

"Pink is just for girls!" my brother says.

Why do some people like pink? Why do some dislike the color?

Let's think about both opinions.

Arguments for Pink Toys

What makes pink different from other colors? People who like pink toys may see no difference. Pink is for everyone, **proponents** say.

Other people may like pink because they think it is a special color. Girls may choose pink toys because they think it is **feminine**, or girlish.

Sometimes toys are pink so they look realistic. Pretend foods such as strawberry ice cream, frosting, shrimp, and ham can be pink.

Stuffed pigs and flamingo puppets are often pink. Why are there pink elephant toys when real elephants are grey?" I wonder.

Some children may have pink bedrooms and want their toys to match their bedspreads and curtains.

Very young children may not know the difference. They are happy playing with toys of all colors.

Children begin to see differences in colors when they are about 18 months old.

Pink toys can help friends and **relatives** choose gifts for girls and boys.

13

Arguments against Pink Toys

Opponents of pink toys argue that they limit girls' choices. Girls may feel they must choose pink.

Girls who don't like pink may feel left out if the toys they like aren't available in other colors.

Boys sometimes think pink is for just girls.

If play kitchens only come in pink, does that **discourage** boys from helping out in a real kitchen?

"Boys like to eat, so why shouldn't they prepare meals and clean up, too?" my friend says.

Toys such as board games that have only pink game pieces may discourage boys from playing.

Pink soccer balls, hula hoops, and baseball bats may keep boys and girls playing **separately**.

Some boys prefer the color pink. Is it fair to only make pink toys for girls?

You Decide

Is it fair to say a color is just for girls or boys?

Would you choose a toy just because it is pink?

Would you avoid playing a game because the ball is pink?

What do you think about pink toys? You can share your thoughts by writing an opinion paper.

Writing Tips

- Tell your opinion first. Use phrases such as:
  - *I like* _____.
  - *I think*_____.
  - _____ *is the best* _____.

- Give many reasons to support your opinion. Use facts instead of stating your feelings.

- Use the words *and, because,* and *also* to connect your opinion to your reasons.

- Explain your facts by using phrases, such as *for example,* or *such as*.

- Compare your opinion to a different opinion. Then point out reasons your opinion is better. You can use phrases such as:
  - *Some people think,* _____ *but I disagree because* _____.
  - _____ *is better than* _____*because* _____.

- Give examples of the positive outcomes of someone agreeing with your opinion. For example, you can use the phrase: *If* _____ *then* _____.

- Include a short story about your own experiences with the topic. For example, if you are persuading someone that the best pet is a dog, you can talk about your pet dog.

- Restate your opinion so your reader remembers how you feel.

Glossary

discourage (dis-KER-ij): try to prevent

feminine (FEM-uh-nin): something with qualities typical of girls or women

opponents (o-PO-nuhnts): people on the other side of a discussion

proponents (pro-PO-nuhnts): people who support something

relatives (REL-uh-tivs): family members

separately (SEP-uh-rate-lee): not together

ndex

Show What You Know

. Name several toys that are pink because the toy maker wants them to look real.

. How might a toy company use the color pink to sell more toys?

. Do you think that pink is a special color just for girls? Why or why not?

Websites to Visit

ww.bbc.uk/schools/ks2bitesize/english/writing/index.shtml

ww.funenglishgames.com/writinggames/debate.html

ww.mindware.com

About the Author

Lin Picou has been teaching for 34 years. She has a master's degree in English Education from the University of South Florida. When she's not in the classroom, she rides her bike and plays baseball with her grandson, Evan.

Meet The Author!
www.meetREMauthors.com

PHOTO CREDITS: Cover (left): ©Jose Manuel Gelphi Diaz; cover (right): ©2p2play; page 1, 4, 7: ©Pavel L Photo& Video; page 5: ©Alina Solovyova-Vincent; page 6, 12: ©Mikhail Tolstoy; page 8: ©CSA-Plastock; page 9: ©iFocus; page 10: ©Cameramannaz; page 11: ©ivolodina; page 13: ©JoeyPhoto; page 14: ©Jorgeprz; page 15: ©Dekanaryas; page 16: ©OZ_Media; page 17: ©RapidEye; page 18, page 19 (right): ©bonnie jacobs; page 18 (right): ©Mega Pixel; page 19: ©Photography1971; page 20: ©Trinacria

Edited by: Keli Sipperley
Cover and Interior design by: Rhea Magaro

Library of Congress PCN Data

Pink Toys, Yes or No/Lin Picou
(Seeing Both Sides)
ISBN (hard cover)(alk. paper) 978-1-63430-346-0
ISBN (soft cover) 978-1-63430-446-7
ISBN (e-Book) 978-1-63430-545-7
Library of Congress Control Number: 2015931674

Printed in the United States of America, North Mankato, Minnesota

Also Available as:

ROURKE'S
e-Books